PRIDE FAMILIES

AMIE TAYLOR

Illustrated by Kaspa Clarke

Jessica Kingsley Publishers
London and Philadelphia

I am Roshni. And this is my family!

I have two mums – Mum and Mãe – mãe means "mum" in Portuguese.

Mum says we are a PRIDE FAMILY. What is a PRIDE FAMILY?

A Pride Family is where one or more parent or carer is LGBTQIA+.

WHAT IS LGBTQIA+?

Lesbian – A woman who is attracted to women.

Gay – A man who is attracted to men or a woman who is attracted to women.

Bisexual – Someone who is attracted to more than one gender.

-Lesbian-   -Gay-   -Bisexual-   -Transgender-   -Queer-   -Intersex-   -Asexual-

Transgender – Someone who does not identify with the sex they were assigned at birth.

Queer – An umbrella term for people who are not heterosexual or cisgender.

Intersex – Someone whose reproductive or sexual parts do not fit the binary definitions of male or female.

Asexual – Someone who experiences little to no sexual attraction to others.

Some kids have two mums, like me!

Some kids have two dads.

And some kids have a mum
and a dad and one of them,
or both of them, are bisexual.

Some kids have a mum who is trans.

Some kids have a dad who is trans.

And some kids have two trans mums, or two trans dads, or a trans mum and a trans dad.

There are so many different ways for Pride Families to look and every way is perfect.

Some kids live with just their dad.

Some kids live with just their mum.

Sometimes this is because their parents are divorced or separated, or because a mum or dad has chosen to have a child or children on their own.

Sometimes a mum or dad might have a boyfriend or girlfriend.

And sometimes a parent is single but they can still be gay, lesbian or bisexual even if they do not have a partner.

Some kids live in families with more than two parents. Sometimes there may be three or four parents.

This may be because a lesbian couple decides to have a baby with a gay couple.

Or because one parent remarries and a child has a step-parent.

There are many reasons someone might have more than two parents.

A step-parent is a parent who is in a relationship with or is married to a child's parent, but who wasn't their parent when they were born.

Some parents are non-binary.

non-binary

If someone is non-binary
it might mean that they
do not identify as being
a man or a woman, or
that they identify with
being both.

A non-binary person may not use the pronouns he/him or she/her. Instead, they may use the pronouns they/them.

Sometimes, a non-binary person may not use "Mum" or "Dad" but prefer to use a different parent name.

Some examples are: Poppy, Baba, Renny, Maddy, Dama and Pari.

There are lots of different ways for parents to have their kids.

In some families the mum is pregnant.

In some families the dad is pregnant.

If a dad is trans it sometimes means that they can have a baby.

Some families adopt their children.   Some families foster their children.

Some families have a surrogate, which means someone offers to carry the baby for them.

To make a baby you need a sperm, an egg and a uterus. My mums each had a uterus and an egg (lots of eggs actually), but no sperm.

Two mums may use an unknown sperm donor to have a baby – this is someone that they may never meet and who may never meet their kids. They simply help to make the baby.

This is how Mum and Mãe had me. I was made using Mum's egg and I grew in Mãe's uterus.

Some families might have a known donor – this is someone that they know who gives them sperm to have the baby but who usually doesn't take on the role of "parent".

Or they might have someone they know who gives them sperm to have the baby and **co-parents** with them once the baby is born.

Co-parenting means parents who all help raise a child together. Some co-parents live together whilst others live separately.

Two dads might adopt or foster their kids, or use a donor egg and have a surrogate, or have a baby with a cisgender woman or a trans man.

And non-binary people have babies too! They might adopt, foster, use a surrogate or have the baby themselves.

Sometimes an LGBTQIA+ person might want a baby but they don't have a partner, boyfriend, girlfriend, spouse, husband or wife.

They might choose to have a baby on their own using a donor sperm or egg, a surrogate, or by adopting.

Even if they don't have a partner, they can still be lesbian, gay or bisexual.

Perhaps you belong to a Pride Family.
Or maybe you have a friend who belongs to a Pride Family?

You may have LGBTQIA+ people in your own family;
aunts, uncles, older siblings, grandparents or guard-/godparents.

There's one final kind of Pride Family, and that's your chosen family – your friends!

I am lucky because Mum and Mãe have loads of chosen family who are all my aunts, uncles, guard-parents and friends. I'm so lucky to have them and love spending time with them.

It's really important to remember that all families are different
and there's no right or wrong way for a family to look.

The most important thing is that every family feels welcomed and included.

NOTES FOR ADULTS

GLOSSARY

Adoption When a child who cannot be looked after by their birth/biological parents goes to live with a new family.

Cisgender Someone who identifies with the sex they were assigned at birth.

Donor A person who provides an egg or sperm so that somebody else can have a baby.

Foster Parent Someone who cares for a child short term if their biological parent/s cannot look after them. It may be while they wait to find an adoptive family, or until they can return to their birth family.

Heterosexual Someone who is attracted to the opposite sex or gender.

Non-binary   Someone who does not identify with binary gender (male/female).

Pride Family   A family that includes one or more parent or caregiver who is not cisgender or/and heterosexual.

Pronoun   Pronouns are what we use to refer to something or someone without using their name. Some examples of pronouns are they, she, he, him, yours, mine.

Surrogate   In pregnancy a surrogate is a person who carries the baby for someone else.

Transgender   A person whose gender identity does not align with the sex they were assigned at birth.

THE DIFFERENCE BETWEEN
GENDER IDENTITY AND SEXUALITY

Although gender identity and sexuality are often talked about together, and are placed together under the acronym LGBTQIA+, they are completely different things.

Your gender identity is your own internal feeling of gender. If you are cisgender the sex you were assigned at birth aligns with the way you experience your gender internally. If you are transgender or non-binary your internal sense of gender is different to the sex you were assigned at birth.

Your sexuality is all about who you are sexually, romantically or emotionally attracted to; whether you are attracted to men, women, men and women, or all genders.

In this book we use lesbian, gay, bisexual and heterosexual to describe sexuality, but there are now many more words including pansexual – meaning attracted to the person regardless of their gender identity. There is also asexuality, which refers to people who do not experience sexual attraction to others (though they may still be in romantic relationships).

POLY RELATIONSHIPS

Although poly relationships are not traditionally listed under the umbrella of LGBTQIA+, an increasing number of LGBTQIA+ (and non-LGBTQIA+) people would describe themselves as polyamorous or non-monogamous – including parents. If someone describes themselves as poly, or in a non-monogamous relationship it means that they are open to and may have romantic relationships and connections with more than one partner. There are many different ways in which non-monogamous relationships may work in families that have children, sometimes secondary or other partners may be involved in a child's life or not.

BISEXUAL OR SINGLE VISIBILITY

With regards to sexuality, if a parent is bisexual but in a relationship with someone of the opposite gender, they may be presumed heterosexual. Likewise, someone may be a part of the LGBTQIA+ community, but a single parent, so their sexuality may not be as clear to see as if they were in a relationship. This doesn't make them any less of a Pride Family – it may not always be clear from the outside, so it's always best to remain open-minded about someone's sexuality, and not make assumptions.

TRANSGENDER PARENTS

Some trans men and non-binary people can carry a baby. Due to this, medical services are making efforts to change language around pregnancy, birth and the fourth trimester to be more inclusive. Chestfeeding replaces breastfeeding and birth person replaces mother.

This forward step in inclusive language is key for ensuring trans and non-binary people feel safe and welcomed when seeking support services around pregnancy and birth.

Some children may still call a trans parent by a gendered name (Mum or Dad) that doesn't align with the parent's gender identity. This can be the case if a parent transitioned after the child was born and of speaking age and is used to calling them by that name. Or the child may adopt a new name for the parent after transition. It is, of course, decided on a family-by-family basis. Respecting and using the name chosen by a parent and their children is key.

ACKNOWLEDGEMENTS

Thank you to Rachel Heilbron, Maggie Saunders, Polly Sheppard, Adam Evans, Simon Pollard, Dan Farrell, Rebecca Rathkey, Neil Harrison, Jamie Turner, Sophia Turner, Annabel, Finlay and Leo.

NOTES